WISE HOMBRE QUIZZES FOR WESTERNERS

by

LANNON MINTZ

Drawings by William Moyers,
member of Cowboy Artists of America

Sunstone Press
Santa Fe, New Mexico

First Edition

Printed in the United States of America

Library of Congress Cataloging in Publication Data:

Mintz, Lannon W., 1938-
  Wise hombre quizzes for westerners / by Lannon Mintz ; drawings by William Moyers.
— 1st ed.   p.   cm.
  ISBN: 0-86534-128-1 : $3.95
  1. West (U.S.) — History — Miscellanea. 2. Cowboys — West (U.S.) — History —
Miscellanea. 3. Frontier and pioneer life — West (U.S.) — Miscellanea. 4. Questions and
answers. I. Title.
F591.M56 1988
978--dc19   88-29437
                                                                     CIP

Published in 1989 by SUNSTONE PRESS
              Post Office Box 2321
              Santa Fe, NM 87504-2321 / USA

FOREWORD

Are you a historian, a wise hombre, lacking in larnin' or a tenderfoot when it comes to western history? Readers of the Westerners International publication, *Buckskin Bulletin*, are familiar with Lannon W. Mintz and his tantalizing quizzes which became a real challenge "to them." Exemplifying what Westerners are all about, Lanny has shared his interest in legends, folklore, facts and trivia affecting the American West. The Albuquerque Corral is indebted to Mintz and his many years of service as a faithful member, secretary and greenback wrangler.

I challenge you to exercise your mental muscles in matching wits and knowledge with this collection of the best of Lanny's western quizzes.

Dr. Don Shockey, Sheriff
Albuquerque Corral, Westerners International

Are you really a wise hombre, or a dude in levis?

Here's a painless way to get a little book larnin' about western history.

Every day — before you saddle ol' Paint and trot off over the horizon — take one of these quizzes. Rate yourself like so:

9 to 10 correct answers, you're a historian

6 to 8 correct answers, you're a wise hombre

3 to 5 correct answers, you're lackin' in book larnin', friend.

0 to 2 correct answers, you're a tenderfoot, Buddy, but keep on tryin'.

Test #1

1. An apishamore is   a. a rope   b. a bull-whip   c. a saddle blanket
2. Butch Cassidy worked in New Mexico at the   a. WS Ranch
   b. Bell Ranch   c. L-C Ranch
3. William Sublette was   a. an outlaw   b. a mountain man
   c. a famous sheriff
4. Hovenweep Monument was home for   a. the Anasazi   b. the
   Hohokam   c. the Mogollon
5. Bishop Lamy died in   a. 1888   b. 1903   c. 1837
6. "Death Valley Scotty's" real name was   a. Scott Johnson
   b. Walter Scott   c. J. Ross Browne
7. Pre-1900 photographers of the west *do not* include   a. Timothy
   H. O'Sullivan   b. William Jackson   c. George Catlin
8. Thomas A. Edison once lived near   a. Gallup, N.M.   b. Golden,
   N.M.   c. Carlsbad, N.M.
9. Robert Olinger was shot by   a. Billy the Kid   b. Doc Middleton
   c. Joel Fowler
10. The Texas ghost town of Terlingua was known for   a. emeralds
    b. quicksilver   c. copper

Test #2

1. Remington's "Turn Him Loose, Bill" recently sold for
   a. $25,000   b. $75,000   c. $175,000
2. Zane Grey's Christian name, before he changed it, was   a. Pearl
   b. Ethelbert   c. Armand
3. *Log of a Cowboy* was written by   a. J. Frank Dobie
   b. Charles Siringo   c. Andy Adams
4. The Bent killed in the Taos uprising of 1847 was   a. William
   b. Charles   c. Silas
5. Charlie Chaplin's movie "The Gold Rush" takes place in
   a. Virginia City   b. The Klondike   c. Sacramento
6. The man held "responsible" for the Mountain Meadows
   Massacre was   a. John Doyle Lee   b. Brigham Young   c. Jacob
   Hamblin
7. Fort Robinson is connected with the death of   a. Sitting Bull
   b. Crazy Horse   c. Satana
8. Cook's Peak is   a. in the Truchas Mts.   b. just west of Socorro
   c. north of Deming
9. New Mexico's "E-Town" was shortened name for   a. Española
   b. Enseñada   c. Elizabeth
10. Probably the "baddest" of these bad gunfighters was   a. Billy
    the Kid   b. John Wesley Hardin   c. Doc Holiday

Test #3

1. Black Jack Ketchum was hanged at   a. Folsum   b. Clayton
   c. Springer
2. The site of Coronado's Bridge (1541) is at   a. Cuchillo   b. Santa
   Fe   c. Puerto de Luna
3. "Long Haired" Jim Courtright was killed by   a. Luke Short
   b. Bat Masterson   c. Ben Thompson
4. The famous *Paso por Aqui* was written by   a. Eugene Rhodes
   b. Uncle Dick Wooten   c. A.B. Guthrie Jr.
5. One of the most mysterious of men, Johnny Ringo, was
   a. Sheriff at Tombstone   b. a Texas Ranger   c. an outlaw
6. Texan Caleb Pirtle is usually associated with   a. music
   b. art   c. law
7. The Paiute "messiah" who championed the Ghost Dance was
   a. Numaga   b. Jack Wilson   c. Wowoka
8. The Colorado River was named by   a. Father Kino
   b. Dominquez and Escalante   c. Father Garces
9. Pueblo Pintado is part of   a. Puye Cliff Dwellings   b. Chaco
   Canyon   c. Mesa Verde
10. The last American Indian to formally surrender to the U.S. was
    a. Sitting Bull   b. Joseph   c. Geronimo

Test #4

1. "Dingus" was the nickname of   a. Frank Sinatra   b. Clay
   Allison   c. Jesse James
2. Fort Union's "sin spot on the Mora" was the nearby town of
   a. Loma Parda   b. San Geronimo   c. Watrous
3. The Spanish Peaks are in   a. a northern Arizona   b. southern
   Colorado   c. northwest N.M.
4. Kit Carson is buried in   a. Fort Garland   b. San Francisco
   c. Taos
5. *Roughing It* was written by   a. Zane Grey   b. Mark Twain
   c. Louie L'Amour
6. Nevada's Walker Lake is named after   a. Gov. Pat Walker
   b. the Walker Indians   c. Joseph R. Walker
7. Brigham Young died in   a. 1806   b. 1912   c. 1877
8. In 1780 you would have found the Cheyenne Indians in
   a. Montana   b. Nebraska   c. Minnesota
9. The Law West of the Pecos was   a. Roy Bean   b. Judge Parker
   c. Charles Goodnight
10. Probably the most famous make of American stagecoach was
    a. Hampshire   b. Boston   c. Concord

Test #5

1. The Grahams and Tewksburys decimated each other in perhaps the west's bloodiest war: a. Lincoln County b. Johnson County c. Pleasant Valley
2. Discoverer of Mesa Verde's Cliff Dwellings was a. Frank Hibben b. Richard Wetherill c. Neil Judd
3. Billy the Kid is buried at a. Lincoln b. Santa Fe c. Fort Sumner
4. The West's most perfectly shaped (extinct) volcano is in northeast New Mexico b. northeast Wyoming c. central Colorado
5. There are approximately_____ Mormons in the U.S. a. 2 million B. 15,000 c. 200,000
6. Wyatt Earp died in a. 1880 b. 1898 c. 1929
7. Prosecuted in the disappearance of Albert Jennings Fountain was a. Pat Garrett b. Oliver Lee c. Billy the Kid
8. That trial was held in a. Santa Fe b. Hillsboro c. Las Cruces
9. Robert Redford's movie "Jeremiah Johnson" was a watered-down portrayal of a. Jim Bridger b. Liver-eating Johnson c. Jed Smith
10. Who wasn't shot in a saloon? a. Doc Holiday b. Wild Bill Hickock c. John Wesley Hardin

Test #6

1. Bill Doolin of the Oklahoma Territory was a. sheriff b. Texas Ranger c. outlaw
2. The river that doesn't have its source in New Mexico, is a. Canadian b. Pecos c. Rio Grande
3. How much of Nevada is federally owned? a. 25% b. 43% c. 86%
4. The number of 14,000 foot mountains in Colorado is a. 55 b. 14 c. 18
5. New Mexico was admitted as the 47th state in a. 1892 b. 1912 c. 1900
6. Samuel Colt invented the six shooter in a. 1859 b. 1800 c. 1836
7. William S. Hart's horse was a. Tony b. Silver c. Fritz
8. Oñate carved his name at Inscription Rock in a. 1605 b. 1710 c. 1751
9. Fort Marcy was in a. El Paso b. Las Cruces c. Santa Fe
10. The Staked Plains are found in a. eastern N.M. b. eastern Okla. c. Texas Panhandle

Test #7

1. Site of the last hostile action by foreign troops inside the Continental United States was   a. Matamoros, Tex.   b. Columbus, N.M.   c. Big Ben, Tex.
2. Guadalupe Mountains National Park is in   a. New Mexico   b. Wyoming   c. Texas
3. The Cheyenne leader killed at the battle of Beecher Island was   a. Roman Nose   b. Sitting Bull   c. Crazy Horse
4. The "Washoe" meant the area around   a. Sacramento   b. Virginia City   c. Idaho City
5. Chief Joseph belonged to the   a. Arapaho   b. Sioux   c. Nez Perce
6. "Doc" Holiday, besides being a gambler and gunman was a   a. veterinarian   b. lawyer   c. dentist
7. First U.S. citizen to go over the deserts and mountains to California was   a. Fremont   b. Lewis and Clark   c. Jed Smith
8. Second explorer to do the same thing was   a. Fremont   b. James O. Pattie   c. Kit Carson
9. Russell, Majors and Waddell were best known for their association with   a. the Pony Express   b. stagecoach lines   c. Wells Fargo
10. Of the Mountain Men, the most famous black was   a. Rose   b. Bridger   c. Beckworth

Test #8

1. "The Cisco Kid" was created by   a. Dobie   b. Owen Wister   c. O'Henry
2. The Indians famous for dancing with live rattlesnakes in their mouths are   a. the Osage   b. the Hopi   c. the Snake
3. The number of Custers killed at the Little Big Horn was   a. one   b. two   c. three
4. "Frijoles" means   a. Hurrah!   b. beans   c. canyon
5. New Mexico author Eugene Manlove Rhodes was   a. State Librarian   b. a cowboy   c. a lawyer
6. The famous lost gold mine "Adams Diggings" is thought by some to be around   a. Magdalena, N.M.   b. Clovis, N.M.   c. Chama, N.M.
7. The Goodnight-Loving Cattle Trail went all the way to   a. Cheyenne   b. Denver   c. St. Louis
8. The "dewlap" on a cow is found   a. under the tail   b. under the head   c. near the privates
9. *Life's Railway to Heaven* was the song sung at the hanging of   a. Henry Plummer   b. Black Jack Ketchum   c. Tom Horn

10. History's most famous mountain crossing, South Pass, is found in which state? a. Montana b. Wyoming c. Colorado

Test #9

1. Sam Ketchum, train robber, is buried a. in Cimarron b. under the Folsum bank c. under N.M. Interstate 25
2. George Catlin was famous as an early Western a. Indian scout b. outlaw c. painter
3. Charles Russell's middle name was: a. Marion b. Monty c. he had none
4. The elevation of the old mining town of Leadville, Colo., is a. 5,280 ft. b. 7, 768 ft. c. 10,200 ft.
5. Saguaro is a. a big cigarillo b. a cactus c. a Mexican border town
6. There are approximately how many separate pieces of leather in a saddle? a. just 3 b. 9 c. 59
7. Sunset Crater is found in a. Colorado b. Utah c. Arizona
8. *The Mustangs* was written by a. Bret Harte b. Zane Grey c. J. Frank Dobie
9. Elbert and Wilson are two of the biggest and most famous mountains in a. Arizona b. New Mexico c. Colorado
10. April 1882 marks the anniversary of the death of a. Sam Bass b. Butch Cassidy c. Jesse James

Test #10

1. Law enforcement officers of Dodge City did not include a. Wyatt Earp b. Wild Bill Hickock c. Bat Masterson
2. Hole-in-the-Wall is found in a. Utah b. Wyoming c. Colorado
3. The only National Park that allows hunting in it, is a. Yosemite b. Grand Teton c. Grand Canyon
4. Independence Rock and Chimney Rock were found along which famous old trail? a. Oregon b. Santa Fe c. Old Spanish
5. The "Hanging Judge" of Indian Territory was a. Judge Roy Bean b. Ambrose Sevier c. Isaac Parker
6. The ghost town of Coloma is found in a. California b. Colorado c. Nevada
7. *Riata and Spurs* was written by: a. William S. Hart b. Gene Autrey c. Charles Siringo
8. The Lost Dutchman Mine is still lost in a. Arizona b. Colorado c. Mexico
9. Tom Mix's horse was named a. Fritz b. Silver c. Tony

10. *Ben Hur* was written by Governor of New Mexico, a. Miguel Otero b. Lew Wallace c. Stephen Kearny

Stage Driver

Test #11

1. Salt Lake City was founded in a. 1847 b. 1801 c. 1863
2. Madrid coal was: a. anthracite b. bituminous c. both
3. Sam Bass was an outlaw from a. Montana b. Arizona
   c. Texas
4. Canyon de Chelly's Navajos were conquered by a. George
   Crook b. Wyatt Earp c. Kit Carson
5. *Luck of Roaring Camp* was written by a. Mark Twain
   b. Bret Harte c. Zane Grey
6. Lewis and Clark went overland in a. 1740 b. 1776 c. 1804
7. Bob Ford died in Creede, Colorado of a. lead poisoning b. old
   age c. consumption
8. Smiley Burnette was mostly the sidekick of a. Gene Autry
   b. Roy Rogers c. Hopalong Cassidy
9. The chuck-wagon was invented by a. Charles Siringo
   b. Charles Goodnight c. Charles Wagon
10. The group most associated the Hasting Cutoff is a. the
    Vigilantes b. the Jayhawkers b. the Donners

Test #12.

1. The city known for having a "Salt War" was
   a. El Paso b. Salt Lake City c. Ogden
2. The old song "Old Paint" is about a. a barn b. Calamity
   Jane c. a horse
3. "McNelley's Rangers" were from a. Colorado b. Texas
   c. Missouri
4. "Jornada" meant a. round-up of horses b. a day's journey
   c. mescal whiskey
5. Women's suffrage is said to have started in which of these
   western ghost towns a. Humbug b. Hell Gate c. South Pass
   City
6. Carrie Nation was a smashing success in a. Oklahoma
   b. South Dakota c. Kansas
7. Fur trappers knew that the only east-west mountain range in
   the Continental U.S. is in a. Arizona b. Oregon c. Utah
8. Wild Bill Hickok was shot from behind by a. Jack McCall
   b. Bob Ford c. Ramon Adams
9. The highest traverse in North America for the last hundred
   years has been a. South Pass b. Mosquito Pass c. Donner Pass
10. Probably the best known bad hombre of California was a. Leo
    Carillo b. Sundance Kid c. Joaquin Murieta

Test #13

1. Frederick Faust is the real name of a. Max Brand b. Zane Grey c. J. Frank Dobie
2. Bent's Fort was located in a. Taos b. the panhandle of Texas c. southeast Colorado
3. The "po-8" stagecoach robber was a. Rube Burrow b. Black Bart c. Bill Carlisle
4. The oldest public building in the U.S. is in a. Philadelphia b. Santa Fe c. Monterey, Cal.
5. Langtry, Texas was the home of a. Judge Roy Bean b. Sam Bass c. Sam Houston
6. The state known as the "Treasure State" is a. Montana b. Utah c. Colorado
7. Gold in Cripple Creek was discovered by a. Marshall Sprague b. Myron Stratton c. Bob Womack
8. In a "tenderloin district" you'd probably see a. a cattle pen b. a meat market c. a red light
9. Marshall Heck Thomas is known for shooting a. Bat Masterson b. Bill Doolin c. John Wesley Hardin
10. Our leading source of arsenic for use in WWI and WWII came from the old mining town of a. Gold Hill, Utah b. Terlingua, Texas c. Ely, Nevada

Test #14

1. To the cowboy, "segundo" meant a. second in charge b. sugar c. a bad man
2. Wyoming Peace Officer Joe Lefors is famous for his capture of a. Crazy Horse b. Frank James c. Tom Horn
3. Nebraska's most famous outlaw was probably a. Doc Middleton b. Ike Stockton c. Jesse James
4. The west's least populated state is a. Wyoming b. Nevada c. Idaho
5. Which is not a well known western artist? a. Harold von Schmidt b. Frank McCarthy c. Ramon F. Adams
6. The first capital of Montana Territory was a. Virginia City b. Helena c. Bannack
7. First white man on the winding Green River was a. William Ashley b. Father Garces c. James O. Pattie
8. First man to really explore the Green River was a. Caleb Greenwood b. Josiah Gregg c. John W. Powell
9. The Hastings Cut-off is part of the a. Santa Fe Trail b. Oregon Trail c. Bozeman Trail

10. The "dirty little coward that shot Mister Howard" was a. Jack McCall b. Ed. O. Kelly c. Bob Ford

Test #15

1. Bodie is a colorful ghost town in a. Montana b. Colorado c. California
2. The famous Elfego Baca shootout took place around a. Creede, Colo. b. Reserve, N.M. c. San Antonio, Texas
3. "Texas Butter" is another name for a. gravy b. a ram c. corn whiskey
4. *Astoria* and *Tour of the Prairies* was written by a. John Jacob Astor b. Mark Twain c. Washington Irving
5. John P. Clum was a. a famous judge b. an Indian agent c. an outlaw
6. Outlaw Curly Bill Brocius came to his unplaned end, courtesy of a. Wyatt Earp b. Hoot Gibson c. Wild Bill Hickok
7. The "Golden State" is a. Colorado b. California c. Alaska
8. "Kid Curry" was the notorious a. Harvey Logan b. Harry Tracy c. Alfred Packer
9. Scotts Bluff is a famous landmark on which overland trail? a. Santa Fe Trail b. Oregon Trail c. California Trail
10. Etta Place is usually associated with a. Jeff Dykes b. Butch Cassidy c. Tom Horn

Test #16

1. Smith, Jackson and Sublette's company was primarily concerned with a. cattle b. fur c. freighting
2. The top cattle state is a. Texas b. Wyoming c. Kansas
3. The "Coyote State" is a. South Dakota b. Nevada c. Wyoming
4. Billy the Kid was shot by a. John Selman b. Wyatt Earp c. Pat Garrett
5. Tiburcio Vasques was well known in California as a a. miner b. bandit c. sheriff
6. Remington and Russell were a. army rifles b. horse thieves c. artists
7. The Northfield, Minnesota bank robbery was the Waterloo for the a. Daltons b. Younger Brothers c. James Brothers
8. Rawhide is a famous ghost town in a. Texas b. Arizona b. Nevada
9. Martha Canary is most likely the real name of a. Willa Cather b. Clamity Jane c. Annie Oakley

10. "Pinto" is a Spanish word meaning   a. beans   b. painted
    c. half-pint

Test #17

1. The 48th state admitted to the Union was   a. New Mexico
   b. Arizona   c. Oklahoma
2. Rot Gut, Humbug Gulch, Sucker Flat and Rough and Ready
   were all mining towns in   a. California   b. Montana
   c. Colorado
3. Gordon Snidow is a well-known western   a. train robber
   b. bronc buster   c. artist
4. "Dinero" means   a. suppertime   b. hat   c. money
5. The well-known Battle of Adobe Walls occurred in the
   a. streets of Laredo   b. Texas Panhandle   c. O.K. Corral
6. "Soapy Smith" was probably the West's best known
   a. detergent salesman   b. con artist   c. philanthropist
7. The Bandit Queen of the Indian Territory was   a. Poker
   Alice   b. Cattle Kate   c. Belle Starr
8. Mescalero, Jicarilla and Chiricahua are all tribes of
   a. Apache   b. Navajo   c. Commanche
9. George F. Ruxton "of the Rockies" is best remembered for
   his   a. writings   b. paintings   c. gunfights
10. "Hard case" Joseph Slade was done in by   a. King Fisher
    b. Thomas Dimsdale   c. the Vigilantes

Test #18

1. An ounce of gold in California in 1849 was worth
   a. $150.00   b. $116.00   c. $16.00
2. To a cowboy, "rattle your hocks" meant   a. travel fast   b. pawn
   everything   c. a snake ahead
3. The "Tall Texan" and the "Sundance Kid" were both members
   of which gang?   a. Daltons   b. Hole-in-the-Wall   c. Vigilantes
4. The colorful Arizona sheriff who, in a shootout, killed three
   men and wounded another in less than a minute was   a. Wild
   Bill Hickok   b. Commodore Owens   c. Bucky O'Neill
5. George Crook was famous as a   a. crook   b. newspaper
   editor   c. soldier
6. Known as the "Equality State" is   a. Wyoming   b. Utah
   c. Oregon
7. The famous book *The XIT Ranch of Texas* was written by   a. J.
   Evetts Haley   b. Charles Siringo   c. J. Frank Dobie
8. Alfred Jacob Miller and Thomas Moran were famous 19th
   Century   a. gunmen   b. artists   c. beer manufacturers

9. Astoria was a fur trading post in   a. British Columbia
   b. Wyoming   c. Oregon
10. The song *Streets of Laredo* is about a   a. dying cow   b. dying
    cowboy   c. romance

Test #19

1. The Bar-20 was the ranch of   a. Charles Siringo   b. Hopalong
   Cassidy   c. Butch Cassidy
2. James Clyman is noted as a famous American   a. artist
   b. sheriff   c. frontiersman
3. John, Jim, Bob and Cole were the outlaw brothers named
   a. James   b. Dalton   c. Younger
4. Former host of the TV series "Death Valley Days" was
   a. Ronald Reagan   b. Walter Brennan   c. Lorne Greene
5. Iron Tail, a Sioux; Big Tree, a Kiowa; and Two Moons, a
   Cheyenne, were used as a composite model for   a. Tonto
   b. the cigar store Indian   c. the Indian nickel
6. Frederick Glidd was the real name of   a. Max Brand   b. Zane
   Grey   c. Luke Short
7. (Here's one to get you thinking) The only state that has never
   been under a foreign flag is   a. Nevada   b. Idaho   c. Oregon
8. *The Celebrated Jumping Frog of Calaveras County* was written by
   a. Mark Twain   b. Robert Louis Stevenson   c. Marshall Sprague
9. The "River of No Return" is the   a. Salmon   b. Green   c. North
   Platte
10. The famous Kentucky Rifle was from   a. Kentucky
    b. Pennsylvania   c. Missouri

Test #20.

1. Gene Autry's horse was   a. Scout   b. Trigger   c. Champion
2. Bell and Olinger were shot by   a. Sam Bass   b. Bass Outlaw
   c. Billy the Kid
3. *Six Guns and Saddle Leather* and *Burrs Under the Saddle"*
   were written by   a. Grizzly Adams   b. Andy Adams
   c. Ramon Adams
4. The ghost town of Shakespeare is found in   a. New Mexico
   b. California   c. Montana
5. "When you call me that, smile!" is the famous line from
   a. Stagecoach   b. The Virginian   c. High Noon
6. El Camino del Diablo (The Devil's Highway) is found in
   a. downtown Los Angeles   b. northern Nevada   c. southern
   Arizona

7. Probably the best known of the Comanches was   a. Sitting Bull   b. Victorio   c. Quanah
8. "Butch" Cassidy's real name was: a. Leroy Cassidy   b. Harvey Longbaugh   c. Robert Parker
9. The Smith River of northern California is the only river named after   a. Whispering Smith   b. Jedediah Smith   c. Soapy Smith
10. Speaking of "Smiths" Joseph Smith was a famous   a. Mormon leader   b. Sheriff of Abilene   c. explorer and trapper

Test #21

1. Alder Gulch is found in   a. Montana   b. Arizona   c. Nevada
2. The Comstock Lode was found in   a. Montana   b. Arizona   c. Nevada
3. The Superstition Mountains, near Phoenix, are noted for   a. the Crazy Swede   b. the Lost Dutchman   c. the Happy Hooligan
4. Wild Bill Hickok played cards for the last time in   a. Cripple Creek   b. Dodge City   c. Deadwood
5. Santa Fe was founded in   a. 1776   b. 1676   c. 1610
6. The horse that survived Custer's Last Stand was named   a. Streak   b. Comanche   c. Soldier
7. Owen Wister wrote   a. The Virginian   b. The Oregon Trail   c. Riders of the Purple Sage
8. "Bronco" Billy Anderson was   a. a rodeo star   b. a Texas outlaw   c. an actor
9. Cimmaron, New Mexico, was for some time, the home of   a. Clay Allison   b. Billy the Kid   c. Dave Rudabaugh
10. Harvey Logan is usually associated with   a. Belle Starr   b. Butch Cassidy   c. Cole Younger

Test #22

1. "Rocky Mountain Canary" is a   a. bald eagle   b. yodeling miner   c. burro
2. Utah is the   a. Palmetto State   b. Equality State   c. Beehive State
3. Most overland pioneers knew the Ruby Mountains were found in   a. Nevada   b. Idaho   c. Colorado
4. Chilkoot Pass is associated with which Gold Rush?   a. the Comstock   b. Klondike   c. 49's
5. Nana, Chato, and Juh were all famous   a. Sioux   b. Navajos   c. Apaches
6. Joe Lefors was a well-known   a. rustler   b. bank robber   c. lawman

7. Marcus Reno is remembered because of the battle at   a. Sand Creek   b. Rosebud   c. Little Big Horn
8. Patrick Gass and John Colter both traveled with   a. Pike   b. Lewis and Clark   c. the Donner Party
9. Which of these fellers was not a famous artist of the West?   a. George Catlin   b. Carl Bodmer   c. Liver-eating Johnson
10. Muriel Wolle and Nell Murbarger wrote about   a. the diet of the Mountain Man   b. ghost towns of the west   c. women gunfighters

Test #23

1. The animal that continues to grow until it dies is the   a. buffalo   b. beaver   c. horse
2. "Sandia" means   a. large house   b. watermelon   c. new mountain
3. The "Beaver state" is   a. Oregon   b. Utah   c. Wyoming
4. Which of the following famous western artist used the drawing of a steer's head in the corner of his paintings as a trademark?   a. Russell   b. Remington   c. Moran
5. The original Boot Hill was found outside of   a. Dodge City   b. Tascosa   c. Denver
6. "Drygulch" refers to   a. an arroyo   b. an ambush   c. a desert town.
7. What remains of the famous Sutro Tunnel is found in   a. eastern California   b. Nevada   c. western Colorado
8. The lesser known, but more interesting, Alpine Tunnel was high up in   a. Kansas   b. Colorado   c. New Mexico
9. Central City, Colo., Virginia City, Nev., and Tombstone, Ariz. are now famous for   a. copper and silver   b. gold   c. tourists
10. Peg Leg Smith was a somewhat famous   a. pirate   b. Sheriff of Dodge City   c. mountain man

Test #24

1. Remember when Alaska became a state?   a. 1949   b. 1956   c. 1959
2. The "Indian Territory" is now the state of   a. Kansas   b. Oklahoma   c. Nebraska
3. What's left of the Alamo is found in   a.Houston   b. Austin   c. San Antonio
4. The best known participant of the Johnson County War was   a. Tom Horn   b. Butch Casidy   c. Bill Hickok
5. One of the best known western artists living today is   a. Bill Moyers   b. John Clyman   c. Thomas Moran

6. Custer's Last Stand took place in   a. Wyoming   b. South Dakota   c. Montana
7. Custer's middle name was: a. Arthur   b. Armstrong   c. Artemis
8. ". . . out where a friend is a friend" is from the song   a. Home on the Range   b. Back in the Saddle   c. Cowboy's Lament
9. Perhaps the West's most famous poet was   a. John Neihardt   b. Zane Grey   c. Grant Foreman
10. Jesse Applegate was a famous   a. dispenser of apple seeds   b. newspaper publisher   c. pioneer

Test #25

1. The top gold producing mine of the U.S. is in   a. South Dakota   b. Colorado   b. California
2. The top gold producing group of mines in the U.S. was at   a. the Mother Lode (Cal.)   b. the Comstock (Nev.)   c. Cripple Creek (Colo.)
3. James Wilson Marshall played a part in the gold strike at   a. the Klondike   b. Goldfield, Nev.   c. the Mother Lode
4. Northfield, Minn. was the Waterloo of which outlaw gang?   a. Younger Brothers   b. Daltons   c. James
5. Baby Doe lived and died in   a. Leadville, Colo.   b. Virginia City, Nev.   c. Tombstone, Ariz.
6. *Sweet Betsy From Pike* is a famous western   a. song   b. painting   c. novel
7. A cowboys "chaps" were his   a. friends from England   b. six guns   c. leather overalls
8. Gambling, legal in Nevada from 1869 to 1910, was legalized again in   a. 1951   b. 1941   c. 1931
9. Pat Garrett is best known for pluggin'   a. John Poe   b. William Bonney   c. Bill Doolin
10. The famous river that ends in the same state it begins in is the   a. Pecos   b. Humboldt   c. Columbia

Test #26

1. The "Centennial State" is   a. Colorado   b. Kansas   c. Wyoming
2. In which of these states do you find the old mining town of Eureka?   a. New Mexico   b. Colorado   c. Nevada
3. Doc Middleton was a well known frontier   a. medic   b. dentist   c. horse thief
4. "Buckshot" Roberts met his demise in which war?   a. Lincoln County   b. Johnson County   c. Pleasant Valley
5. The Espinosa gang executed their dastardly deeds in   a. Colorado   b. Arizona   c. Texas

6. ". . . where seldom is heard a discouraging word" is from the song a. The Last Roundup b. Streets of Laredo c. Home on the Range
7. Judge Roy Bean's "court room" was on the . . . a. Chisum Trail b. Texas Border c. Red River
8. The "hoosegow'" of the West was a. a rodeo b. jail c. hobbling a horse
9. One of the earliest accounts of the fur trade is by a. John Bartlett b. Zenas Leonard c. William H. Jackson
10. William Manly is remembered for his heroism at a. Pike's Peak b. Death Valley c. The Alamo

Test #27

1. "Father of the Santa Fe Trail" is the title given to a. Kit Carson b. George Bent c. William Becknell
2. The Blackfoot Indians would have most likely chased you out of a. Montana b. New Mexico c. Kansas
3. Wild Bill Hickok's real name was a. William Settle Hickok b. William James Hickok c. James Butler Hickok
4. Jackson Hole, Wyoming is named after a. David Jackson b. Andrew Jackson c. William H. Jackson
5. Shot dead in Deadwood was a. Calamity Jane b. Wild Bill Hickok c. Jesse James
6. "With a banjo on my knee" is from the song a. Sweet Betsy from Pike b. Oh, Susannah! c. The Last Roundup
7. Monument Valley, the site of at least four dozen Hollywood westerns, is in a. Utah b, Wyoming c. Arizona
8. Captain Bonneville is known for his early 19th Century a. travels b. Indian campaigns c. rodeos
9. Roy Rogers' horse was called a. Champion b. Scout c. Trigger
10. When a cowboy "passed in his chips" he was usually a. collecting buffalo droppings b. playing poker c. dead

Test #28

1. Catherine Antrim was mother of a. Butch Cassidy b. Billy the Kid c. Jesse James
2. Elizabeth Bacon became famous because of her husband a. Robert Browning b. George Custer c. Tom Eggs
3. The romantic interest of Butch Cassidy and the Sundance Kid was a. Calamity Jane b. Etta Place c. Lotta Crabtree
4. The state that had much to do with the ladies getting to vote was a. Wyoming b. Texas c. Utah

5. Sacagawea is remembered as a   a. writer b. guide c. gun runner
6. Esmeralda County, home of many ghost towns such as Gold Point and Goldfield is in   a. California b. Colorado c. Nevada
7. Probably the west's most famous female "Jessie" was the wife of   a. John Fremont b. Jesse James c. Frank James
8. Juanita Brooks and Mari Sandoz are well known western a. horse-thieves b. artists c. historians
9. Probably the first white woman to cross the Rockies was a. Belle Starr b. Narcissa Whitman c. Mrs. Donner
10. The Dolores River flows in   a. Nebraska b. Oregon c. Colorado

Test #29

1. One of the great Apache leaders was   a. Victorio b. Captain Jack c. Manuelito
2. "Woodchuck" is another name for a   a. marmot b. beaver c. wolverine
3. Probably the most famous lynching of a "lady" was of   a. Belle Starr b. Madame Mustache c. Cattle Kate
4. *Riders of the Purple Sage* was written by   a. Jack London b. Stuart Lake c. Zane Grey
5. Texas's baddest "bad" man was probably   a. John Wesley Hardin b. Sam Bass c. Bill Doolin
6. The Yampa is a   a. mountain b. river c. desert
7. Site of the west's first gold rush was   a. Cherry Creek, Colo. b. Cerrillos, N.M. c. Coloma, Calif.
8. Sheep ranching was probably introduced in this country by a. Charles Goodnight b. Tom Horn c. Oñate
9. ". . . we'll come back again when we've panned out a pile" is from the famous song   a. Oh, Susannah! b. Bury Me Not on the Lone Prairie c. Sweet Betsy from Pike
10. First cowboy star to sing western songs in the movies was a. Ken Maynard b. Hoot Gibson c. Gene Autry

Test #30.

1. In the movies "America's Favorite Cowboy" was the title of a. Roy Rogers b. Gene Autry c. Johnny Mack Brown
2. Speaking of Johnny Mack Brown, anybody remember his horse? a. Black Nell b. Remo c. Buck
3. The Wind River is found mostly in   a. Wyoming b. Utah c. Idaho

4. The outlaw who had a brother "Frank" was a. Cole Younger b. Tiburcio Vasquez c. Jesse James
5. The "Buntline Special" was used by a. Wyatt Earp b. Butch Cassidy c. "Pistol Pete" Petura
6. Crazy Horse was killed at a. The Little Big Horn b. Wounded Knee c. Fort Robinson
7. "Pompey's Pillar" is a landmark associated with a. Mark Twain b. Lewis and Clark c. Clarence King
8. The tune played by the band as Custer's troops marched from the fort for the last time was a. Round Her Neck She Wore a Yellow Ribbon b. The Girl I left Behind Me c. Dixie
9. *Paso Por Aqui* was written by a. Eugene Manlove Rhodes b. Bret Harte c. A.B. Guthrie Jr.
10. You can still drive the Million Dollar Highway in a. Colorado b. Los Angeles c. The Yukon

Test #31

1. A latïgo is found a. in a bottle b. on a saddle c. in a gold mine
2. John Deere is best known for designing a a. wagon b. tractor c. plow
3. "Founding Father of Texas" was a. Stephen Austin b. Sam Houston c. Sam Bass
4. The old town of Bannack is found in a. Montana b. Idaho c. Colorado
5. John Wayne's real first name was a. Duke b. Michael c. Marion
6. The man whose death started the Lincoln County War was a. Albert Jennings Fountain b. John Chisum c. John Tunstall
7. "Kid Antrim" was an alias for a. William Bonney b. Billy the Kid c. Henry McCarty
8. Elfego Baca was a famous New Mexico a. author b. bandito c. lawman
9. Most famous of all Kiowas was probably a. Santana b. Gall c. Geronimo
10. The meeting place for the first transcontinental rail line was at a. Denver, Colo. b. Topeka, Kan. c. Promontory, Ut.

Test #32

1. The state flower of Nevada is a. sagebrush b. daisy c. rose
2. The Reno Brothers were a. founders of Reno b. outlaws c. professional gamblers

3. The wild and wooly town of Tascosa was found in
   a. southeast Arizona   b. New Mexico   c. Texas
4. A "parfleche" is a   a. hide   b. gambler   c. French perfume
5. Jim Baker was a well known   a. outlaw   b. sheriff   c. trapper
6. Governor Lew Wallace took office in   a. 1897   b. 1878   c. 1917
7. Meriweather Lewis was a famous   a. artist   b. politician
   c. explorer
8. The Bill Williams River flows in   a. Arizona   b. Colorado
   c. Wyoming
9. *Two Years Before The Mast* was written by   a. Father
   Kino   b. Father Escalante   c. Richard Dana Jr.
10. Bob Steele was an early day   a. Governor of New Mexico
    b. movie star   c. outlaw

Test #33

1. Bernard DeVoto is best known as a   a. fur trapper   b. artist
   c. writer
2. The Big Rock Candy Mountain can be found in   a. Utah
   b. New Mexico   c. fiction only
3. Sontag and Evans were early   a. insurance agents
   b. outlaws   c. songwriters
4. Mangus and Chatto were well-known member of which tribe?
   a. Navajo   b. Crow   c. Apache
5. A "llano" is a   a. Spanish horse   b. prairie   c. loner
6. Here's a tougher one: a "hooley-ann" involves   a. cattle
   rustling   b. sheep rustling   c. roping
7. "He stole from the rich and gave to the poor" is a line from the
   song   a. Streets of Laredo   b. Sam Bass   c. Jesse James
8. Which of these men *was not* an artist of the Old West?
   a. Albert Bierstadt   b. George Catlin   c. William H. Jackson
9. Dave McCanles' noted death was sure a big help to the
   notoriety of   a. Hickok   b. Kit Carson   c. Billy the Kid
10. The "Sunflower State" is   a. Arizona   b. Wyoming   c. Kansas

Test #34

1. Death Valley Scotty was famous for   a. his fast draw   b. his
   lost mine   c. his fast women
2. The biggest river flowing in Teton National park is
   a. Snake   b. Green   c. Moose
3. Calamity Jane claimed a "relationship" with   a. Wild Bill
   Hickok   b. Bat Masterson   c. the 7th Cavalry
4. Charlie Russell's stompin' grounds were mostly   a. Montana
   b. Idaho   c. Kansas

5. A "pinto" horse is one that is   a. small   b. bean fed   c. spotted
6. Which of these states was admitted to the Union *first*?
   a. Nevada   b. Nebraska   c. North Dakota
7. The Choctaw "Land of the Red People" is   a. South Dakota
   b. Wyoming   c. Oklahoma
8. One of the West's real brave men, Tom Smith, was a
   a. sheriff   b. fur trapper   c. explorer and surveyor
9. The picturesque old mining town of Mogollon is found in
   a. southern Arizona   b. west Texas   c. southern New Mexico
10. The man who explored the Grand Canyon and climbed its walls
    with just one arm was   a. Escalante   b. Muir   c. Powell

Chief

Test #35

1. The world's first train robber was a. Jesse James b. Black Jack Ketchum c. John Reno
2. Long's Peak is now part of which park? a. Glacier b. Yosemite c. Rocky Mountain
3. The Old West's unofficial record of 12 spouses belongs to a. Custer b. Liver-eating Johnson c. Calamity Jane
4. When someone is "buffaloed", they are a. confused b. surrounded c. running
5. The Fremont Expedition that ended disasterously in Colorado's frozen mountains was his a. first b. thirty-first c. fourth
6. The famous scout accompanying Fremont on that expedition was a. Bill Williams b. Kit Carson c. Jed Smith
7. Considered the best of Idaho's ghost towns is a. Garnet b. Silver City c. South Pass City
8. Ben K. Green is one of the West's most entertaining a. bunco artists b. writers c. rodeo stars
9. The lady who starred in "Duel In the Sun" was a. Greer Garson b. Jane Wyman c. Jennifer Jones
10. A first edition of Lewis and Clark's "Expedition" costs about a. $50.00 b. $10,000 c. $500.00

Test #36

1. The well-known river that flows through Big Bend National Park is a. Pecos B. Rio Grande c. Rogue
2. It couldn't be the Rogue, you say, because that's in a. Oregon b. Utah c. Nebraska
3. The Colorado and Green Rivers meet in which National Park? a. Yellowstone b. Canyonlands c. Yosemite
4. The river that flows through Death Valley is a. there is none b. Mojave c. Amagosa
5. The original Ft. Union was located on which river? a. Missouri b. Mississippi c. Colorado
6. The original fur trade river route was on the a. Snake b. Missouri c. Colorado
7. The Gibbon, Firehole and Snake are all rivers found in a. Sun Valley b. Yellowstone Park c. Rocky Mountain Park
8. The famous "Jornada del Muerto" comes close to which river? a. Des Chutes b. Gila c. Rio Grande
9. The "River of No Return" runs through the middle of a. Washington b. Oregon c. Idaho
10. Described as "a thousand miles long and six inches deep" is the a. Humboldt b. Platte c. Canadian

1. A Rocky Mountain "canary"   a. cackles   b. tweets   c. brays
2. The famous Army Post, Fort Bowie, is located in   a. New Mexico   b. Arizona   c. Texas
3. If you soaked your pinkies in the Crazy Woman Creek, you'd be in   a. Wyoming   b. Colorado   c. Kansas
4. The aloe and maguey plants are used in making (hic)   a. Mescal   c. tequila   c. rye
5. (Here's an easier one) The Judith Mountains are in   a. Texas   b. Montana   c. Kansas
6. The only major military post with a woman's name, Fort Henrietta, was destined for obscurity in   a. Nevada   b. Oregon   c. Arizona
7. The ghost town of Lulu City was found in   a. Yosemite   b. Rocky Mountain Park   c. Montana
8. The woman most responsible for the 18th Amendment may well have been   a. Mrs. Warren G. Harding   b. Isabella Bird   c. Carrie Nation
9. A "strumpet" is a   a. women's horn   b. orchestra member   c. soiled dove
10. Elizabeth McCourt Tabor is better remembered as   a. Poker Alice   b. Belle Starr   c. Baby Doe

1. Dominguez and Escalante originally called it the San Buenaventura River; it is now known as the   a. Colorado   b. Green   c. Rio Grande
2. The National Monument of Scotts Bluff is in   a. Nebraska   b. Wyoming   c. Kansas
3. Pierre Jean DeSmet was an early   a. missionary   b. sheriff   c. vigilante
4. The name "Beadle" is associated with the late 1800's   a. singing groups   b. carriages   c. dime novels
5. Thomas Fitzpatrick, mountain man, guide, and Indian agent was called   a. Deerslayer   b. Broken Hand   c. Cut Nose
6. The first U.S. post in Arizona, Ft. Defiance, was to control the   a. Apache   b. Navajo   c. rustlers
7. "Ursus arctos horribilus" is the   a. beaver   b. grizzly   c. burro
8. One of Albuquerque's most famous writers is   a. C.L. Sonnichson   b. Leroy Hafen   c. William Keleher
9. The Dirty Devil River is flowing in   a. Utah   b. Arizona   c. California

10. The first great explorer(s) in North America. . . a. Lewis and Clark b. MacKenzie c. Z. Pike

Test #39

1. Alfred Packer is reported to have eaten five of Hinsdale County's seven a. horses b. aspens c. democrats
2. The Maroon Bells are found near a. Aspen b. San Jose c. Santa Fe
3. Olive Oatman is best remembered as a a. bandit b. "entertainer" c. captive
4. The famous book *Commerce of the Prairies* concerns which trail? a. Bozeman b. Santa Fe c. Oregon
5. "Forty rod" usually refers to a. distance b. whiskey c. a bad farm
6. The Coeur d'Alene is found in a. Oregon b. Idaho c. Kansas
7. The "Strauss" of the California gold rush produced a. Viennese waltzes b. beer c. pants
8. ". . . from where the sun now stands, I will fight no more forever" are the famous words of a. Geronimo b. Chief Joseph c. Custer
9. The "unsinkable Molly Brown" was an early day a. aircraft carrier b. swimmer c. socialite
10. Butch Cassidy held up the bank in a. Salt Lake City b. Tombstone c. Telluride

Test #40

1. The woman who wrote *Wake of the Prairie Schooner; a retracing of the Oregon Trail,* was a. Belle Starr b. Juanita Brooks c. Irene Paden
2. Lake Elenor is found in which Park? a. Glacier b. Yosemite b. Yellowstone
3. Didn't do too well on that one eh? How about St. Marys Lake, you should know it's in a. Glacier b. Yosemite c. Yellowstone
4. In the early west "foofaraw" meant a. a wife b. dried beef c. fancy dress
5. "Fuzz-tail" referred to a. a sportin' gal b. a horse c. an unclear story
6. Elizabeth Bonduel McCourt was better known as a. Molly Brown b. Calamity Jane c. Baby Doe Tabor
7. Another famous "Elizabeth" was the wife of a. Custer b. Fremont c. Seldom Seen Slim

8. A "cut-nose squaw" was one caught in   a. the turkey
   a. carving   b. snooping   c. adultery
9. That big ole mama bear is really a member of which family?
   a. horse   b. dog   c. opossum
10. "Mother Carey's Chickens" referred to a   a. bacon and egg
    breakfast   b. bad egg   c. strumpet

Test #41

1. "Captain Jack" Crawford was a well known   a. artist   b. Indian
   chief   c. poet
2. In his later life he was in charge at Ft. Garland, Colo., he
   was   a. Kit Carson   b. George Crook   c. Nelson Miles
3. The picturesque town at the "Switzerland of America" is
   a. Jackson, Wy.   b. West Yellowstone   c. Ouray, Colo.
4. The Wapatki Indian ruins are found in   a. Utah   b. northern
   Arizona   c. southern Arizona
5. The last name of the outlaw "Blackjack" was   a. Ketchum
   b. Christian   c. Dealer
6. Robert Redford's movie "Jeremiah Johnson" was based on the
   book   a. The Big Sky   b. Crow Killer   c. Life in the Rocky
   Mountains
7. "Cibolero" refers to a   a. type of grass   b. buffalo hunter
   c. outlaw
8. The novel, The Virginian, was written by   a. Zane Grey
   b. Owen Wister   c. Max Brand
9. One of the West's best ghost towns, Elkhorn, is in
   a. Montana   b. Wyoming   c. Colorado
10. Here's one for you architects: The term Victorian indicates
    a. a style   b. a period of time   c. a non-ornate structure

Test #42

1. The mountain man known as "Old Gabe" was   a. Kit
   Carson   b. Jim Bridger   c. Bill Williams
2. The spectacular Mission Mountain range is found in
   a. Colorado   b. California   c. Montana
3. Gen. George Crook called them "tigers of the human race"
   a. Apache   b. Navajo   c. Sioux
4. "Smoke of a .44", "A Bronc to Breakfast", and "The Broken
   Rope" are all examples of the paintings of   a. Remington
   Russell   c. Bill Moyers
5. The "oxbow route" was another name for which trail?
   a. Butterfield   b. Mormon   c. Oregon

6. Ft. Fetterman was established on which trail?   a. Butterfield
   b. Bozeman   c. California
7. Fetterman and eight of his soldiers were wipe out by Sioux
   led by   a. Crazy Horse   b. Sitting Bull   c. Gall
8. 1869 saw the birth of the first transcontinental   a. stagecoach
   line   b. mail service   c. railroad
9. Chris Madsen was well known in the Oklahoma and Indian
   Territories as a   a. killer and outlaw   b. lawman   c. pioneer
   preacher
10. The 1873 Winchester, "the gun that won the West" was so-
    called because   a. it was a 15-shot repeating rifle   b. the lever
    ejected the old shell and replaced it with a new one   c. it's
    bullets could also be used in the Colt pistol

Test #43

1. To a cowpoke a "snuffy" was   a. tobaccy   b. a cook   c. a wild
   horse
2. In the Old West an Arkansas toothpick was a   a. skinny kid
   from Little Rock   b. walking cane   c. knife
3. A "baile" was   a. money to get outta jail   b. a load of cotton
   c.a dance
4. "Poncho" was a   a. Mexican revolutionary   b. friend of the
   Cisco Kid   c. blanket you could wear
5. In a six horse team the horses in the middle were the   a. swing
   team   b. leaders   c. wheelers
6. "Tinhorn" was usually used to describe a   a. sheriff
   b. gambler   c. tenderfoot
7. The Russian thistle is better known as   a. yucca   b. Khrushchev
   cactus   c. tumbleweed
8. "Bumblebee whiskey" was rotgut that   a. "came with a
   sting"   b. was made from bees   c. you drank with your honey
9. A "jacal" was   a. a wild dog   b. a jacal of all trades   c. a hut
10. A cantina was a   a. bandito   b. horse   c. tavern

Test #44

1. The tongue of a buffalo is   a. red   b. black   c. white
2. An average rabbit lives about _____years?   a. two
   b. six   c. twenty
3. The "double eagle" gold piece was worth   a. $20   b. $10
   c. $100
4. The President who owned a famous ranch in the Dakotas
   was   a. Teddy Roosevelt   b. Harry Truman   c. Millard Fillmore

5. Only four actors in western have won Oscars. They are:
   a. "In Old Arizona" (1928-29) _____
   b. "High Noon"   (1952)   _____
   c. "Cat Ballou"   (1965)   _____
   d. "True Grit"   (1969)   _____
6. The Spanish Peaks are found in   a. Texas   b. New Mexico
   c. Colorado
7. The woman who was put in the Yuma jail was   a. Calamity
   Jane   b. Pearl Hart   c. Rose of the Cimarron
8. The famous author of *Rattlesnakes*, *The Mustangs*, and *Voice of the Coyote* was   a. J. Frank Dobie   b. A.B. Guthrie
   c. Louis L'Amour
9. He died of pneumonia in 1909:   a. Wyatt Earp   b. Kit
   Carson   c. Geronimo
10. The western city with the most sunshine in a year is
    a. Phoenix   b. Sacramento   c. Albuquerque

Test #45

1. The longest river in the U.S. is the   a. Missouri
   b. Mississippi   c. Colorado
2. 134 degrees, hottest ever recorded in the U.S., was at   a. Death
   Valley, Calif.   b. Presidio, Texas   c. Gila Bend, Arizona
3. The Ruby Mountains are found in   a. Texas   b. Nevada
   c. Colorado
4. The rifle was carried on which side of the saddle?   a. right
   b. left   c. either
5. The shoot-out at Rock Creek Station, Nebraska, made whose
   reputation?   a. Quantrill   b. Wild Bill Hickok   c. Jesse James
6. The well known ghost town of Rhyolite is in   a. Nevada
   b. California   c. Utah
7. "Drag rider" was a cowboy who   a. dressed funny   b. rode old
   "drags" and "nags"   c. followed the last cow
8. Al "Fuzzy" St. John would most likely be the sidekick of   a. Bat
   Masterson   b. Kit Carson   c. Ken Maynard
9. If you visited the Mandan Tribe around 1840, you'd be in
   a. Idaho   b. Kansas   c. North Dakota
10. Alfred V. Kidder was a well known   a. painter
    b. archeologist   c. sculptor

Test #46

1. The frontier woman prepared most of the family soap by
   a. crushing the root of the common yucca   b. mixing melted
   rendered lard and lye   c. combining the inner bark of the locust
   tree, wood ash, and boiling water

2. The famous woman guide of the Lewis and Clark Expedition was of the a. Snake Indian Tribe b. Crow Indian Tribe c. Shoshone Indian Tribe

3. Prairie marble refers to the building material used in contructing the a. dugout home b. adobe house c. sod shanty

4. The famous statue dedicated to pioneer women which was sculptured and erected by Robert Gage is located in a. Casper, Wyoming b. Ardmore, Oklahoma c. Topeka, Kansas

5. Cow chips refers to a. dried cow manure used for fuel b. the crust which formed on butchered meat c. an infection of cattle hooves caused by walking on wet ground.

6. Indian women made a concentrated food that was called pemmican which consisted of a. corn meal and dried berries boiled and dried b. pine nuts and honey which were ground together and baked c. lean dried meat pounded fine and mixed with melted fat

7. The major target of the WCTU which achieved real cohension in the 1870's was a. the elimination of alcoholic beverages b. the achievement of women's suffrage c. the introduction of religious revivals in all male dominated societies

8. The authoress of *No Life For a Lady* resided in the vicinity of a. Fort Union, N.M. b. Lincoln, N.M. c. Datil, N.M.

9. Concepcion and Jamie were two major characters found in a western book entitled a. *Riders to Cibola* b. *Under the Wide Sky* c. *Black Range Tales*

10. During the pioneer days, Christmas trees were decorated with a. small china figures b. construction paper chains c. strings of popcorn and cranberries

Test #47.

1. A catamount is a a. wildcat b. weapon c. silver measure

2. The first United States "I Want You" poster featured a. Tom Mix b. William S. Hart c. Teddy Roosevelt

Cowboy

3. The WWA (Western Writers of America) selected as best novel   a. *The Virginian*   b. *Shane*   c. *Ox-bow Incident*
4. Author of *Destry Rides Again* is   a. Max Brand   b. Zane Grey   c. Luke Short
5. Why and Ben Hur are places in   a. Arizona   b. Nevada c. fiction only
6. Phoebe Ann Moses was the real monicker of   a. Calamity Jane   b. Muriel Wolle   c. Annie Oakley
7. In 1850 a "rocker" in California was   a. an ancient Beach Boy   b. long haired miner who sang a lot   c. cradle for washing gold
8. David Thompson is a famous western   a. explorer   b. artist c. outlaw
9. The famous "Lost Adams Diggins" are reportedly around a. Zuni, N.M.   b. Pima, Arizona   c. Butte, Montana
10. The first big gold camp established after gold was found in Calif. was   a. Old Dry Diggins   b. Hangtown   c. Placerville

Test #48

1. Anybody out there remember this word, "ramsquaddle?" It meant   a. sit on a sheep   b. big spender   c. defeat
2. How about this word: If a woman suffered from a nervous disorder???   a. treble   b. peedoodles   c. tremolos
3. How about this: An important man was caled a   a. ripstaver b. bounder   c. rouge
4. Long ago a strong man was referred to as a   a. montropolous b. screamer   c. brute
5. Many men knew that to "cheat with false love" was to a. forsake   b. woo   c. honeyfogle
6. Well for those of you who believe action speaks louder than words outlaw Ben Kilpatrick, the "Tall Texan" was a well known member of which gang?   a. Doolin   b. Wild Bunch c. Younger Brothers
7. Independence Rock is a famous landmark on the ____ Trail. a. Oregon   b. Bozeman   c. Santa Fe
8. The first state to enact homestead legislation was   a. Texas b. Nebraska   c. Kansas
9. Choctaw, Chickasaw, Cherokees and Senaca Indians all once lived in today's   a. Nebraska   b. Colorado   c. Oklahoma
10. Vulture, one of the West's best, but least known ghost towns is in   a. Arizona   b. Nevada   c. Wyoming

1. "Going to the Sun" road is found in   a. Colorado
b. California   c. Montana
2. The number of Colorado peaks over 10,000 feet is about
a. 15   b. 150   c. 1500
3. The number of people now living in California is about   a. 25
million   b. 10 million   c. 2 million
4. Montana, about the same size, has   a. less than a million
b. 3 million   c. six million
5. Guadalupe National Park is in   a. Texas   b. Arizona   c. New
Mexico
6. The famous frontiersman that lived in Taos, N.M., was   a. Kit
Carson   b. George Bent   c. Uncle Dick Wootton
7. The natural wonder featured in the movie "Close Encounters of
the Third Kind" was   a. Bo Derek   b. Devils Monument   c. The
Grand Tetons
8. The most famous Mormon cowboy was probably   a. Brigham
Young   b. Butch Cassidy   c. Will Bill Hickok
9. T. O'Sullivan was a well known early   a. Irish boxer
b. photographer   c. painter
10. "Pa-Ha-Sa-Pa" is the Indian name for   a. Mt. Hood   b. The
Grand Canyon   c. The Black Hills

Test #50

1. The former Texas Governor James Hogg named his daughter
a. Ima   b. Lotta   c. Petunia
2. The number of Indians in the Civil War was about
a. 10,000   b. 10   c. 1000
3. A "tapadero" is found on a   a. saddle   b. dancer's shoes
c. barfly
4. The National Monument with no road in to it is   a. Gran
Quivera   b. Rainbow Bridge   c. Devil's Tower
5. The Mountain Meadows Massacre took place in
a. Montana   b. Idaho   c. Utah
6. Perhaps the most famous name associated with the massacre
was   a. Oliver Lee   b. John Doyle Lee   c. Lee Marvin
7. Court-martialed in 1867 was   a. Gen. Phil Sheridan
b. Geronimo   c. Custer
8. Probably the most cluttered, over-commercialized National Park
is   a. Glacier   b. Yellowstone   c. Yosemite
9. The Canadian, Pecos, and Mimbres Rivers all flow in
a. Arizona   b. New Mexico   c. Texas

10. "A way, we've found a way . . ." is a line from the song
    a. Dying Cowboy b. Lil Joe the Wrangler c. Shenandoah

Test #51

1. Congress prohibited the killing of bison in
   a. 1941 b. 1894 c. never
2. Roy Rogers made his last singing western in a. 1952
   b. 1962 c. 1972
3. The man who did the most for the National Park System
   was a. John D. Rockefeller b. Abraham Lincoln
   c. Teddy Roosevelt
4. Berlin, Osceola and Tuscarora all are ghost towns in
   a. Nevada b. California c. Colorado
5. The most famous opera about mining camp life was "Girl
   of the Golden West" by: a. Dvorak b. Puccini c. Aaron
   Copeland
6. On May 17, 1873 the big news in Albuquerque, Texas was
   the shooting of well-known Jack Helms by a. Billy the
   Kid b. John Wesley Hardin c. Stephen F. Austin
7. The classic western, *The Life of John Wesley Hardin*, was
   written by a. himself b. J. Frank Dobie c. John Selman
8. The Cliff Palace is found in a. Mesa Verde b. Chaco
   Canyon c. Hearst Castle
9. The Louisiana Purchase cost the United States a. 50
   million b. 15 million c. 150 million
10. Henry Plummer's gang of outlaws, gunmen and road
    agents was called the a. Innocents b. Hole-in-the-Wall
    Gang c. Exterminators

Test #52

1. Catherine Antrim was related to a. Lewis and Clark
   b. Calamity Jane c. Billy the Kid
2. Helena, Mont. was once known as a. Last Chance Gulch
   b. Brewery Gulch c. First Chance Gulch
3. Nevada's Humboldt River was once called a. Alice's
   b. Mary's c. St. Helen's
4. Narcissa Whitman was a a. pioneer missionary b. dance hall
   madam c. female sheriff
5. She was also one of the first women to a. dance the kootch-koo
   in Leadville b. scalp an Indian c. cross the Rocky Mountains
6. The greatest obstacle to women's suffrage, according to Susan
   B. Anthony, was a. "short sighted men" b. "long sighted
   men" c. the apathy of women

7. A "basque " is a   a. cleansing in a French tub.   b. child lacking a legal pop   c. sheepherder
8. Maiden is a ghost town in   a. Taiwan   b. Montana   c. Texas
9. Public law 92-195 was passed in 1971 to protect the West's 8,000   a. wild women   b. wild burros   c. wild rivers
10. Calamity Jane's horse was   a. Flower   b. Buttercup   c. Satan

Test #53

1. A century and a half ago "kinnikinnick" was   a. the hiccups   b. relative   c. tobacco
2. "Lady-broke" was a description of a   a. destitute woman   b. hen-pecked cowboy   c. gentle horse
3. Levis were known for   a. damming up rivers   b. copper rivets   c. early fashion
4. Nose paint, tanglefoot, and bug juice were all   a. southwest flora   b. Indian war paint   c. liquor
5. A "lobo" was a   a. basketball player   b. railroad bum   c. timber wolf
6. Mañana meant   a. tomorrow   b. sometime   c. perhaps never
7. Watch this one! A moncho was a   a. heavy dude   b. massive snack   c. animal missing part of his anatomy
8. A "Monkey Ward" cowboy was a   a. mental case   b. real swinger   c. mail order devotee
9. A "rocker" was a   a. long haired guitar player   b. miner of granite   c. short trough for gold
10. "Bushwhack" was   a. to flail with flora   b. sticky substance from weeds   c. to lie in wait for

Test #54

1. Betrayed by a pal, this famous outlaw was killed in 1878 at Round Rock, Texas. He was   a. Sam Bass   b. Doc Holliday   c. Bat Masterson
2. Born in New York, he came west with his widowed mother and lived in Silver City, New Mexico in the 1860's . . .   a. Black Jack Ketchum   b. Tom Horn   c. Billy the Kid
3. One-time lawmen, they tried to rob two banks simultaneously. . .   a. Daltons   b. Youngers   c. James Brothers
4. He borrowed the name of a friend who trained him to be a rustler   a. Butch Cassidy   b. Billy the Kid   c. Bill Doolin
5. Owner of a violent, erratic nature, he died falling from a wagon   a. Frank James   b. Clay Allison   c. Wyatt Earp
6. At one time a scout for the Army and a Pinkerton agent, he was   a. John Wesley Hardin   b. Tom Horn   c. Wild Bill Hickok

7. She participated in this country's last stagecoach holdup. . .
   a. Belle Starr b. Pearl Hart c. Silver Dollar Tabor
8. This member of the Wild Bunch had $40,000 in rewards on
   him a. Kid Curry b. Sundance Kid c. "Big Nose" George
   Curry
9. A jovial Arkansas farmhand and a member of the Dalton Gang,
   he was a. Happy Hooligan b. Bill Doolin c. Roy Bean
10. Using the name Tom King, she dressed as a man and became
    Bob Dalton's mistress, her name was a. Flo Quick c. Clammy
    Jane c. Belle Starr

Test #55

1. The epitome of the mountain man, "Old Gabe" was a. William
   Ashley b. Jim Bridger c. Kit Carson
2. Castoreum was used to attract a. buffalo c. beaver c. comely
   squaw
3. A Hawken rifle could kill a griz or buffler at a. 100 ft. or
   less b. 100 yards c. 200 yards
4. Most likely the largest of all trading forts in the West was a. Ft.
   Bridger b. Ft. Bent c. Astoria
5. The first large group of emigrants headed west was led by
   trapper a. "Broken Hand" Fitzpatrick b. Manuel Lisa c. Old
   Bill Williams
6. The beaver trade business died about a. 1920 b. 1840
   c. 1860-65
7. The famous trapper who travelled with the Lewis and Clark
   party was a. John Colter b. Jed Smith c. William Ashley
8. Jackson Hole, Wy., was named for a. David Jackson
   b. Andrew Jackson c. William H. Jackson
9. "Uncle Dick" Wootton, famous frontiersman, lived near
   a. Taos b. Raton c. Santa Fe
10. The greatest explorer among the fur trappers was, without a
    question, a. Jedediah Smith b. Jim Bridger c. Joseph R.
    Walker

Test #56

1. The Yellowstone River joins the Missouri in a. Wyoming
   b. North Dakota c. Montana
2. The term "looking over his shoulder" usually meant a. on the
   dodge b. learnin' by watching c. severe neck injury
3. Author of Smokey, Cowboys North and South, and
   The Drifting Cowboy was a. Jesse James b. Will James
   c. Henry James

4. The Mormon church (LDS) was officially organized in which state? a. Utah b. Illinois c. New York
5. The name Las Vegas means a. meadows b. lose a lot c. timbers
6. The Colorado River has it source in which National Park? a. Colorado b. Rocky Mountain c. Yellowstone
7. Outlaw Charles E. Bolten was better known as a. White William b. Black Bart c. Ringo
8. Retail costs of the original Concord Stagecoach was a. $15,000 b. $7,124,92 c. ¢1050
9. Which of the following did not become a state until after the Civil War? a. Oregon b. Kansas c. Montana
10. Stovepipe Wells is found in a. California b. the Grand Canyon c. Bryce Canyon

Mountain Man

1. Today the inside of a bourbon barrel is   a. painted blue
   b. charred   c. tarred.
2. By 1900 women were allowed to vote in how many states?
   a. 4   b. 14   c. 21
3. The Sacagawea statue in Portland was dedicated in 1905 by
   a. Gloria Steinham   b. Susan B. Anthony   c. Sacagawea
4. The western classic, *The Land of Little Rain,* was written by
   a. Jane Astor   b. Mary Austin   c. William Manly
5. In 1890, Emma Green was the first woman to design a state seal
   for   a. Idaho   b. New Mexico   c. Kansas
6. The West was notorious for attracting _____women.
   a. religious   b. short   c. non-conforming
7. The ghost towns of Alma and Elizabethtown are found in
   a. California   b. Utah   c. New Mexico
8. Bourbon is made mostly of   a. wheat   c. barley   c. corn
9. Fanny Kelly and Olive Oatman were both   a. women outlaws
   b. soiled doves   c. Indian captives
10 Home of the only round courthouse still in use is at   a. Santa
   Fe, N.M.   b. Lovelock, Nevada   c. Casper, Wyoming

1. General Custer is buried at   a. the Little Big Horn   b. West
   Point   c. the Black Hills
2. A "waddy" was a   a. chaw of tobacco   b. cowboy   c. pregnant
   cow
3. The rugged Black Rock Desert is found in   a. Arizona
   b. Nevada   c. Utah
4. Speaking of Utah: one river *not* found there is the
   a. Yampa   b. Fremont   c. Beaver
5. The monument to a jackass is found at   a. Santa Fe, N.M.
   b. Fairplay, Colo.   c. Skagway, Alaska
6. In 1970, the population of Sun Valley, Idaho was   a. 317
   b. 31,700   c. 317,000
7. John Mix Stanley made his name in   a. steamers   b. finding
   Livingstone   c. painting
8. Little Crow, Red Cloud, and Crazy Horse were all
   a. Cheyenne   b. Sioux   c. Crow Indians
9. Guadalupe Peak is the highest mountain in   a. Texas
   b. Okalahoma   c. California
10. The state flag of Wyoming features a white   a. flower
   b. buffalo   c. eagle

Test #59

1. Another name for the "Ox Bow Route" was   a. Butterfield Trail   b. Santa Fe Trail   c. Bozeman Trail
2. Pony Express mail from St. Joseph, Mo. to Sacramento took about   a. 10 days   b. 20 days   c. 30 days
3. Today a letter from St. Joe to Sacramento takes   a. 10 days   b. 20 days   c. occasionally forever
4. How old was Wm. F. Cody when he was a pony express rider?   a. 15   c. 25   c. approaching 40
5. The western classic *Roughing it* was written by   a. Sam Clemens   b. John Fremont   c. Charlie Russell
6. The Cheyenne chief who escaped at Sand Creek was   a. Black Kettle   b. Black Elk   c. Red Cloud
7. A cow that ate snakeroot reportedly resulted in   a. death by locoweed   b. milk sickness   c. foot and mouth disease
8. A "tapadero" protects the   a. boot   b. six gun   c. neck
9. Thomas Hart Benton was the "father" of   a. the Gadsden Purchase   b. Texas independence   c. Manifest Destiny
10. A "careta" was an early   a. cigar   b. cart   c. water container

Test #60

1. When Columbus arrived, the Sioux Indians lived in   a. South Dakota   b. Texas   c. North Carolina
2. Blazers Mills was an important aspect of which war?   a. the Civil   b. Johnson County   c. Lincoln County
3. Gila monsters carry a reserve supply of food in their   a. nose   b. skin   c. tail
4. The all-time box office (Western) champ is   a. Billy Jack   b. Butch Cassidy and Sundance Kid   c. High Noon
5. Some unpolite hombres claim Calamity Jane had how many husbands?   a. 5   b. 8   c. 12
6. The Mormon faith was founded in   a. New York   b. Illinois   c. Utah
7. The book *Two Years Before the Mast* was written by   a. Father DeSmet   b. Father Dyer   c. Richard Dana
8. A "plew" in the old west was a   a. bad smell   b. seat in church   c. beaver pelt
9. Seldom Seen Slim was a famous (well, almost famous)   a. donkey   b. prospector   c. early dietician
10. Once buffalo land, Nebraska now has approx. ____ farms?   a. 70,000   b. 7,000   c. 700

1. "Buckshot" Roberts was one of the many casualties of the ____war
   a. Civil b. Lincoln County c. First World
2. To an Indian "moon" meant a. night b. obscene gesture
   c. month
3. The Lolo Trail winds through much of a. Arizona b. Idaho
   c. Colorado
4. The Lolo's most famous travellers were a. the Dalton
   Brothers b. Lewis and Clark c. soiled doves
5. Wayne Brazel confessed to the shooting of a. President
   Garfield b. Pat Garrett c. Meriweather Lewis
6. "Colter's Hell" refers to a. Devil's Postpile b. Devil's
   Tower c. Yellowstone
7. O.C. Seltzer is famous for his a. water b. paintings c. horses
8. Alexander McSween was done in at a. Casper, Wyoming
   b. Bodie, Calif. c. Lincoln, N.M.
9. Before Mt. St. Helens, the last eruption in the western states
   was a. Mt. Rainier b. Mt. Whitney c. Lassen Peak
10. Remember Charles Starrett? In the movies he was a. Wild Bill
    Hickok b. the Durango Kid c. Kit Carson

Test #62

1. The emigrant crossing of the Truckee River became known
   as a. Reno b. Carson City c. Las Vegas
2. The different number of species of rattlesnakes in the U.S. is
   a. 3 b. 5 c. 15
3. The state with the most species of same is a. Arizona
   b. Florida c. Texas

Stage Robber

39

4. The West's second largest lizard is the   a. whiptail
   b. chuckwalla   c. gila
5. The General responsible for the Sand Creek Massacre was
   a. Miles   b. Chivington   c. Custer
6. In Alberta, there really was a Fort   a. Whoopincough
   b. Whoop-de-do   c. Whoop-up
7. The explorer who almost froze in the Colorado mountains
   was   a. Fremont   b. Pike   c. Jed Smith
8. _____ was not shot into a permanent state in a saloon
   a. Wild Bill   b. John Wesley Hardin   c. Sam Bass
9. The famous trapper killed by Indians was   a. Jed Smith
   b. Broken Hand Fitzpatrick   c. Jim Bridger
10. When miners danced, the one with the handkerchief was
   a. ailing   c. a brow mopper   c. a lady

Test #63

1. The highest waterfall in the U.S. is in which National Park
   a. Yellowstone   b. Yosemite   c. Rocky Mountain
2. The highest bridge is in   a. Colorado   b. California   c. Arizona
3. How many miles long is Grand Canyon?   a. 71   b. 217   c. 117
4. In the old west a "remuda" was a   a. string tie   b. hat   c. string
   of horses
5. John Mix Stanley was a famous   a. movie cowboy
   b. explorer   c. painter
6. The famous old mining town of Hillsboro is found in
   a. Colorado   b. New Mexico   c. Arizona
7. Quanah Parker was a famous   a. Comanche   b. Sioux
   c. Arapaho
8. The Lipan Indians were of what tribe?   a. Apache
   b. Shoshoni   c. Cheyenne
9. As sheriffs go, this feller was fairly well known   a. Charles
   Siringo   b. John Slaughter   c. O.C. Seltzer
10. If you spot a grizzly 200 yards away you should probably
   a. sing your death song   b. run like h———   c. not move

Test #64

1. The first large scale success of irrigation outside of Utah was
   at   a. Greeley, Colo.   b. Santa Fe, N.M.   c. Pocatello, Idaho
2. The Black Rock Desert is found in   a. Oregon   b. Nevada
   c. Idaho
3. The state with the largest percentage of farmlands is
   a. Nebraska   b. Texas   c. Montana

4. William Antrim was really a. Billy the Kid b. Henry McCarty c. William Bonney
5. Wheeler Peak is found in a National Park in a. Utah b. California c. Montana
6. Who was told to "Hang on to the Matchless"? a. H.A.W. Tabor b. Augusta c. Baby Doe
7. The "Matchless" can still be seen in a. Cripple Creek b. Creede c. Leadville
8. In old New Mexico a "muchacha" is a a. dance b. hot pepper c. girl
9. Ansel Adams is perhaps best known for his photos of a. Grand Canyon b. Yosemite c. Yellowstone
10. Montezuma's Castle was built by a. Montezuma b. Sinagua Indians c. Apaches

Test #65

1. The opposite of a "bonanza" was called a a. floppo b. folly c. borrasca
2. In 1870 you would have run into the Modoc Indians in a. California b. Modoc, Oklahoma c. Modoc, Texas
3. Watch this one: the Red River is found in a. New Mexico b. Utah c. Texas
4. An experienced prospector was called a a. high grader b. sourdough c. miner
5. The gunfighter who could (so they say) quote Shakespeare: a. Butch Cassidy b. Billy Younger c. Johnny Ringo
6. Here's another tricky: the Canadian river is found in a. Calgary b. Oklahoma c. New Mexico
7. The famous old town and fort, Fort Steele is found in a. Utah b. Arizona c. British Columbia
8. Helena (Montana) was originally: a. Lousetown b. Last Chance Gulch c. Hangtown
9. An area not included in the Louisiana Purchase was a. New Mexico b. North Dakota c. Idaho
10. George Drouillard is usually assoicated with a. Jesse James b. Lewis and Clark c. Cripple Creek, Colo.

Test #66

1. A rose is a member of which family? a. mesquite b. cactus c. lily
2. Killed in an attack on Toronto was the western explorer a. John Bartlett b. Zebulon Pike c. John Fremont

Law Man

3. Hangtown was at the end of the _____ trail.
   a. Oregon b. Bozeman c. California
4. Henry Plummer was Montana's most famous a. sanitary engineer b. fruit grower c. outlaw
5. The world's largest buffalo is in a. No. Dakota b. Wyoming c. Kansas
6. The Huge Pyramid (Ames Monument) is found in which state? a. Iowa b. Texas c. Wyoming
7. Seems like the hottest it ever got around a thermometer out West was at a. Yuma b. Death Valley c. Terlingua, Texas
8. The "Beehive" State is a. Utah b. Nebraska c. So. Dakota
9. That last one was sorta easy, how about the "Gem" State? a. Nevada b. Oregon c. Idaho
10. The mining techniques of the Gold Rush were probably inherited from a. Colorado b. Ohio c. Georgia

Test #67

1. Which country first created National Parks? a. Sweden b. U.S. c. England
2. What percent of Alaska is federally owned? a. 99% b. 66% c. 33%
3. Cabrillo National Monument is found in a. Arizona b. Texas c. California
4. James Fennimore Cooper was the creator of a. Hawkeye b. Natty Bumpo c. Pathfinder
5. Gold in California was first discovered on which river? a. Sacramento b. American c. Yuba
6. The first state pensions for the elderly were introduced by which states? a. Kansas and Nebraska b. Wyoming and Montana c. California and Oregon
7. Of the 254 counties in Texas, oil has been found in a. 211 b. 21 c. 99
8. The man most responsible for Geronimo's surrender was a. George Crook b. Tom Horn c. Kit Carson
9. The Spanish word "cibola" meant a. buffalo b. a short rope c. prairie grass
10. Rough and Ready was a well-known mining town of a. Colorado b. Nevada c. California

Test #68

1. The Washoe is found in a. Washington b. Nevada c. Oregon
2. Our newest National Park is found in a. Washington b. Nevada c. Oregon

3. Owyhee Country is found in   a. Hawaii   b. California   c. Idaho
4. Convicted of shooting Sheriff William Brady was   a. Billy the Kid   b. Clay Allison   c. Belle Star
5. A "quirt" is a   a. little guy   b. soft drink   c. riding whip
6. The Lochsa and the Little Salmon Rivers are found in a. Idaho   b. Nevada   c. Colorado
7. "Man from Snowy River" is a western taking place in a. Hawaii   b. Australia   c. China
8. A ghost town not to miss seeing in Montana is   a. Silver City   b. Bakerville   c. Elkhorn
9. Pancho Griego was shot by: a. Billy the Kid   b. Joel Fowler c. Clay Allison
10. Composer of the famous ballet "Rodeo" is   a. Richard Wagner   b. Leonard Bernstein   c. Aaron Copland

Test #69

1. The Grand Canyon rattlesnake feeds on   a. birds   b. tourists c. rodents
2. The tarantula feeds on   a. unfaithful wives   b. spiders c. insects
3. You have to climb to Balcony House at   a. Mesa Verde b. Chaco Canyon   c. Hovenweep
4. Speaking of Hovenweep, it's found way out in the desert of a. Arizona   b. Utah   c. New Mexico
5. Walter Scott is usually associated with   a. Death Valley b. Ivanhoe   c. Yosemite
6. John Muir was famous as a   a. painter   b. poet   c. naturalist
7. Doc Middleton was a well known   a. surgeon   b. podiatrist c. outlaw
8. Doc Holliday was a well known   a. optometrist   b. dentist c. outlaw
9. Holliday was a victim of   a. the Gunfight at O.K. Corral b. T.B.   c. old age.
10. El Capitan at 8,078 feet is the highest point in   a. California b. Texas   c. Wyoming

CORRECT ANSWERS

1.) 1-c, 2-a, 3-b, 4-a, 5-a, 6-b, 7-c, 8-b, 9-a, 10-b
2.) 1-c, 2-a, 3-c, 4-b, 5-b, 6-a, 7-b, 8-c, 9-c, 10-b
3.) 1-b, 2-c, 3-a, 4-a, 5-c, 6-b, 7-b & c, 8-c, 9-b, 10-c
4.) 1-c, 2-a, 3-b, 4-c, 5-b, 6-c, 7-c, 8-c, 9-a, 10-c
5.) 1-c, 2-b, 3-c, 4-a, 5-a, 6-c, 7-b, 8-b, 9-b, 10-a
6.) 1-c, 2-c, 3-c, 4-a, 5-b, 6-c, 7-c, 8-a, 9-c, 10-a & c
7.) 1-b, 2-c, 3-a, 4-b, 5-c, 6-c, 7-c, 8-b, 9-a, 10-c
8.) 1-c, 2-b, 3-c, 4-b, 5-b, 6-a, 7-a, 8-b, 9-c, 10-b
9.) 1-c, 2-c, 3-a, 4-c, 5-b, 6-c, 7-c, 8-c, 9-c, 10-c
10.) 1-b, 2-b, 3-b, 4-a, 5-c, 6-a, 7-c, 8-a, 9-c, 10-b
11.) 1-a, 2-c, 3-c, 4-c, 5-b, 6-c, 7-a, 8-a, 9-b, 10-c
12.) 1-a, 2-c, 3-b, 4-b, 5-c, 6-c, 7-c, 8-a, 9-b, 10-c
13.) 1-a, 2-c, 3-b, 4-b, 5-a, 6-a, 7-c, 8-c, 9-b, 10-a
14.) 1-a, 2-c, 3-a, 4-a, 5-c, 6-c, 7-a, 8-c, 9-b, 10-c
15.) 1-c, 2-b, 3-a, 4-c, 5-b, 6-a, 7-b, 8-a, 9-b, 10-b
16.) 1-b, 2-a, 3-a, 4-c, 5-b, 6-c, 7-b, 8-c, 9-b, 10-b
17.) 1-b, 2-a, 3-c, 4-c, 5-b, 6-b, 7-c, 8-a, 9-a, 10-c
18.) 1-c, 2-a, 3-b, 4-b, 5-c, 6-a, 7-a, 8-b, 9-c, 10-b
19.) 1-b, 2-c, 3-c, 4-a, 5-c, 6-c, 7-b, 8-a, 9-a, 10-b
20.) 1-c, 2-c, 3-c, 4-a, 5-b, 6-c, 7-c, 8-c, 9-b, 10-a
21.) 1-a, 2-c, 3-b, 4-c, 5-c, 6-b, 7-a, 8-c, 9-a, 10-b
22.) 1-c, 2-c, 3-a, 4-b, 5-c, 6-c, 7-c, 8-b, 9-c, 10-b
23.) 1-b, 2-b, 3-a, 4-a, 5-a, 6-b, 7-b, 8-b, 9-c, 10-c
24.) 1-c, 2-b, 3-c, 4-a, 5-a, 6-c, 7-b, 8-b, 9-a, 10-c
25.) 1-a, 2-c, 3-c, 4-a, 5-a, 6-a, 7-c, 8-c, 9-b, 10-b
26.) 1-a, 2-c, 3-c, 4-a, 5-a, 6-c, 7-b, 8-b, 9-b, 10-b
27.) 1-c, 2-a, 3-c, 4-a, 5-b, 6-b, 7-a & c, 8-a, 9-c, 10-c
28.) 1-b, 2-b, 3-b, 4-a, 5-b, 6-c, 7-a, 8-c, 9-b, 10-c
29.) 1-a, 2-a, 3-c, 4-c, 5-a, 6-b, 7-b, 8-c, 9-c, 10-a
30.) 1-b, 2-b, 3-a, 4-c, 5-a, 6-c, 7-b, 8-b, 9-a, 10-a
31.) 1-b, 2-c, 3-a, 4-a, 5-c, 6-c, 7-a, b, & c, 8-c, 9-a, 10-c
32.) 1-a, 2-b, 3-c, 4-a, 5-c, 6-b, 7-c, 8-a, 9-c, 10-b
33.) 1-c, 2-a, 3-b, 4-c, 5-b, 6-c, 7-c, 8-c, 9-a, 10-c
34.) 1-b, 2-a, 3-a, 4-a, 5-c, 6-a, 7-c, 8-a, 9-c, 10-c
35.) 1-c, 2-c, 3-c, 4-a, 5-c, 6-a, 7-b, 8-b, 9-c, 10-b
36.) 1-b, 2-a, 3-b, 4-c, 5-a, 6-b, 7-b, 8-c, 9-c, 10-b
37.) 1-c, 2-b, 3-a, 4-a, 5-b, 6-b, 7-b, 8-c, 9-c, 10-c
38.) 1-b, 2-a, 3-a, 4-c, 5-b, 6-b, 7-b, 8-c, 9-a, 10-b
39.) 1-c, 2-a, 3-c, 4-b, 5-b, 6-b, 7-c, 8-b, 9-c, 10-c
40.) 1-c, 2-b, 3-a, 4-c, 5-b, 6-c, 7-a, 8-c, 9-b, 10-c

41.) 1-c, 2-a, 3-c, 4-c, 5-a & b, 6-b, 7-b, 8-b, 9-a, 10-b
42.) 1-b, 2-c, 3-a, 4-b, 5-a, 6-b, 7-a, 8-c, 9-b, 10-a, b & c
43.) 1-c, 2-c, 3-c, 4-c, 5-a, 6-b, 7-c, 8-a, 9-c, 10-c
44.) 1-b, 2-b, 3-a, 4-a, 5-a-Warner Baxter, b-Gary Cooper,
c-Lee Marvin, d-John Wayne, 6-c, 7-b, 8-a, 9-c, 10-b
45.) 1-b, 2-a, 3-b, 4-c, 5-b, 6-a, 7-c, 8-c, 9-c, 10-b
46.) 1-b, 2-a, 3-c, 4-c, 5-a, 6-c, 7-a, 8-c, 9-a, 10-c
47.) 1-a, 2-b, 3-a, 4-a, 5-a, 6-c, 7-c, 8-a, 9-a, 10-a, b & c
48.) 1-c, 2-b, 3-a, 4-b, 5-c, 6-b, 7-a, 8-a, 9-c, 10-a
49.) 1-c, 2-c, 3-a, 4-a, 5-a, 6-a, 7-b, 8-b, 9-b, 10-c
50.) 1-a, 2-a, 3-a, 4-b, 5-c, 6-b, 7-c, 8-c, 9-b, 10-c
51.) 1-b, 2-a, 3-c, 4-a, 5-b, 6-b, 7-a, 8-a, 9-b, 10-a
52.) 1-c, 2-a, 3-b, 4-a, 5-c, 6-c, 7-c, 8-b, 9-b, 10-c
53.) 1-c, 2-c, 3-b, 4-c, 5-c, 6-a, b & c, 7-c, 8-c, 9-c, 10-c
54.) 1-a, 2-c, 3-a, 4-a, 5-b, 6-b, 7-b, 8-a, 9-b, 10-a
55.) 1-b, 2-b, 3-c, 4-b, 5-a, 6-b, 7-a, 8-a, 9-b, 10-a
56.) 1-b, 2-a, 3-b, 4-c, 5-a, 6-b, 7-b, 8-c, 9-c, 10-a
57.) 1-b, 2-a, 3-b, 4-b, 5-a, 6-c, 7-c, 8-c, 9-c, 10-b
58.) 1-b, 2-b, 3-b, 4-a, 5-b, 6-a, 7-c, 8-b, 9-a, 10-b
59.) 1-a, 2-a, 3-c, 4-a, 5-a, 6-a, 7-b, 8-a, 9-c, 10-b
60.) 1-c, 2-c, 3-c, 4-b, 5-c, 6-a, 7-c, 8-c, 9-b, 10-a
61.) 1-b, 2-c, 3-b, 4-b, 5-b, 6-c, 7-b, 8-c, 9-c, 10-b
62.) 1-a, 2-c, 3-a, 4-b, 5-b, 6-c, 7-a, 8-c, 9-a, 10-c
63.) 1-a, 2-a, 3-b, 4-c, 5-c, 6-b, 7-a, 8-a, 9-b, 10-c
64.) 1-a, 2-b, 3-a, 4-a, b & c, 5-c, 6-c, 7-c, 8-c, 9-b, 10-b
65.) 1-c, 2-a, 3-a & c, 4-b, 5-c, 6-b, & c, 7-c, 8-b, 9-c, 10-b
66.) 1-b, 2-b, 3-c, 4-c, 5-a, 6-c, 7-b, 8-a, 9-c, 10-c
67.) 1-b, 2-a, 3-c, 4-a, b & c, 5-b, 6-b, 7-a, 8-a, 9-a, 10-c
68.) 1-b, 2-b, 3-c, 4-a, 5-c, 6-a, 7-b, 8-c, 9-c, 10-c
69.) 1-c, 2-c, 3-a, 4-b, 5-a, 6-c, 7-c, 8-b & c, 9-b, 10-b

About the Author:

Lannon Mintz has traveled the western states extensively, taking photographs to illustrate lectures, and doing research on his book, *The Trail, A Bibliography of Travelers on the Overland Trail, 1841-1884*, published by University of New Mexico Press, 1987.

Lanny and Linda Mintz have lived in Albuquerque since 1962, and he has been a member of Albuquerque Corral of Westerners for the past fifteen years, most of that time serving as treasurer, newsletter editor and quiz originator.

Lanny's professional life is in the news media, having spent seven years as an announcer and almost twenty years as sales manager at a major Albuquerque station, and over a year with a large television station. He served one term as President of the Albuquerque Broadcasting Association.

About the Artist

William T. Moyers lived on a ranch in Colorado since he was a young boy, where, perhaps, he developed a taste for western subjects. He has lived in Georgia and Massachusetts, and still maintains a home in Pagosa Springs, Colorado as well as Albuquerque, N.M. He has won honor and recognition both for his paintings and his bronzes. He has belonged to the Cowboy Artists of American for many years, has served three times as president, and has won numerous awards for his sculptures in their annual shows. His work is represented in museums and galleries throughout the southwest and Rocky Mountain west.

On August 5, 1988 while this book was being prepared for publication, the author, Lannon Mintz, died. Though he did not live to see the finished book, he knew it was being published, and was happy about it. The Albuquerque Corral of Westerners International dedicates this book to Lanny's memory with affection and respect. Lanny had a lot of fun writing these quizzes; we hope you have as much fun reading and answering them.

www.ingramcontent.com/pod-product-compliance
Lightning Source LLC
Chambersburg PA
CBHW031154090426
42738CB00008B/1331